Tigers

Kate Riggs

CREATIVE EDUCATION

seedlings

Published by Creative Education
P.O. Box 227, Mankato, Minnesota 56002
Creative Education is an imprint of
The Creative Company
www.thecreativecompany.us

Design by Ellen Huber
Production by Chelsey Luther
Art direction by Rita Marshall
Printed in the United States of America

Photographs by Corbis (Randy Wells), Dreamstime (Tiago
Estima, Isselee), Getty Images (Thorsten Milse, Stephen Ennis
Photography), iStockphoto (Ryan Lusher, TheBiggles, Pierre
van der Spuy), Shutterstock (Iakov Filimonov, Eric Isselée,
dominique landau, Michal Ninger, red-feniks, Valentijn
Tempels, Ultrashock, worldswildlifewonders), SuperStock
(Biosphoto, Juniors, Minden Pictures)

Library of Congress Cataloging-in-Publication Data
Riggs, Kate.
Tigers / Kate Riggs.
p. cm. — (Seedlings)
Includes index.
Summary: A kindergarten-level introduction to tigers,
covering their growth process, behaviors, the habitats they call
home, and such defining physical features as their striped fur.
ISBN 978-1-60818-344-9
1. Tiger—Juvenile literature. I. Title.

QL737.C23R5395 2013
599.756—dc23   2012027070

First Edition
9 8 7 6 5 4 3 2 1

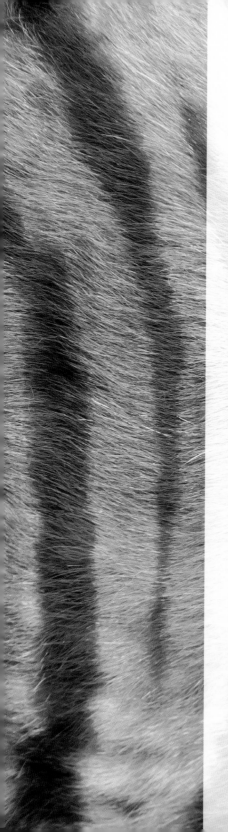

TABLE OF CONTENTS

Hello, tigers!

Tigers are big
cats that roar.

They live in Asia.

Tigers have striped fur.

Tigers are orange or white. Their stripes are black.

Tigers have big teeth. They have sharp claws on their paws.

Tigers eat meat.
They hunt deer
and wild pigs.
Some tigers eat
monkeys.

A baby tiger is called a cub. Cubs live with their mother. Adult tigers live alone.

Tigers like to
sleep during
the day. They
look for food
at night.

Goodbye, tigers!

Picture a Tiger

ears

nose

teeth

whiskers

claws

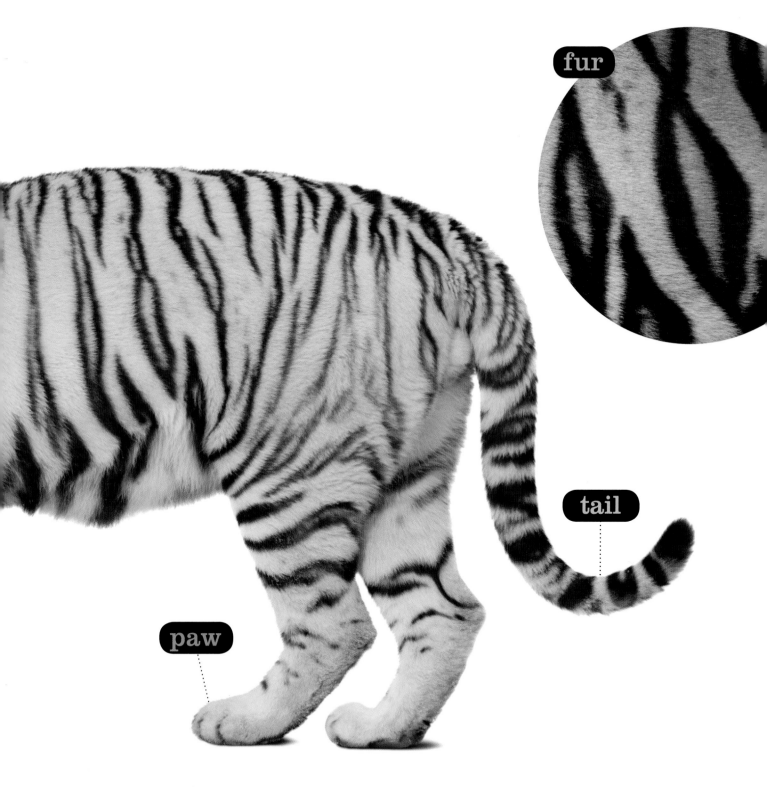

fur

tail

paw

21

Words to Know

Asia: the biggest piece of land in the world

claws: curved, pointed nails on the paw

fur: the short, hairy coat of an animal

Read More

Marsh, Laura. *Tigers*.
Washington, D.C.: National Geographic Society, 2012.

Thomson, Sarah L. *Amazing Tigers!*
New York: HarperCollins, 2004.

Websites

DLTK's Jungle Tigers
http://www.dltk-kids.com/animals/jungle-tigers.html
Make a tiger craft. Or print out pictures to color.

Folding Paper Zoo Animals
http://www.firstpalette.com/Craft_themes/Animals/Folding_
Instructions/Folding_Instructions.html
Have an adult help you make a tiger out of paper!

Index